Quick & Easy

VIETNAMESE
HOME COOKING
FOR EVERYONE

ANDRÉ NGUYEN
YUKIKO MORIYAMA

BOUTIQUE-SHA,INC.

Distributors

United States: Kodansha America, LLC. through Oxford University Press, 198 Madison Avenue, New York, NY 10016, U.S.A.

Canada: Fitzhenry and Whiteside, 195 Allstate Parkway, Markham, Ontario, L3R 4T8.

Asia and other countries: Japan Publications Trading Co., Ltd., 1-2-1, Sarugaku-cho, Chiyoda-ku, Tokyo 101-0064, Japan

Co-published by Japan Publications Trading Co., Ltd. and Boutique-sha, Inc.

6th Printing January 2010

Printed in Japan
ISBN: 978-4-88996-125-6

ACKNOWLEDGMENTS

We wish to express our heartfelt gratitude to many people far and near
for their invaluable assistance in the making of
"VIETNAMESE HOME COOKING FOR EVERYONE".

First we would like to acknowledge and give warm thanks
to our publisher, BOUTIQUE-SHA,INC., Shiro Shimura for his trust and faith in our work;
to Vice President, editor in Chief, Akira Naito, who kindled our enthusiasm and got the project going ;
Yoshihiko Koshizuka, whose photographic talents are readily evident
as being of the highest caliber;
Koji Abe, Yoko Ishiguro, Mieko Baba whose editiorial assistance,
and their hard work and dedication are much appreciated,
and have been keys to the success of our project;
Masako Sekimoto, Keiko Yanagihara, Memi Ishikawa
whose secretarial help was much appreciated;
Tom Brooke, whose writing ability
was indespensable for making English language complexities simple;
Kazuto Narahara, whose patient and careful book promotion plan
are much appreciated.

We are indebted to you all including staff at Andre's Eurasian Bistro for your support,
encouragement and patience for the completion of this project.

Lastly, my personal thank you to my devoted parents
Anh Nguyen and Huong Ding, especially
my mother who passed on to me her ability and passion
for home cooking and the desire to share this gift with others;
my loving wife Noël Tu for the continued understanding and support;
my son Huy for all his help on this project.
His computer skills and tasting ability were invaluable;
my young children Veronica and Dunstan
for always being there for me, helpful and loving;
my brothers for their support at the beginning of my career
that has continued unwavering to this day.

CONTENTS

CONTENTS

INTRODUCTION

Vietnam is a country of natural beauty with a coastline of sandy beaches stretching about 2000 miles (3225 km) from the northern to the southern tip of the South China Sea. Along the coast, fishing is the main livelihood.

The majority of Vietnamese people are Kinh race people (87%) with the remaining of 53 different ethnic minority groups.

For more than 2000 years, the country has been subjected to a near continuing series of foreign occupations from China, France, Japan, and America. One consequence of these occupations is the lasting influence on Vietnamese cuisine.

Among Vietnamese dishes, perhaps the best known in the West is *Pho*, a noodle soup. Another is the deep-fried spring roll called *Nem* in the north, and *Cha Goi* in the south. Rice is a staple food used as a side dish, or a main dish when combined with other ingredients, such as beef, pork, chicken, or seafood. Vietnamese dishes consist of many different blends of herbs and spices. Most dishes are not fiery hot, nor greasy. Seafood and vegetarian dishes like *An Chay* are very popular. Today, Vietnamese cuisine is gaining increased international attention due to the fact that it is quite healthy.

This book is an introduction to a new generation for a delicious journey through Vietnamese cuisine. While the combination of flavors may seem experimental to some, they will result in a savory experience. All ingredients used in these recipes can be found in supermarkets, natural food stores or in Asian food markets. It is our pleasure to share these quick and delicious Vietnamese recipes with you. Enjoy the good nutrition that comes with it.

MAP OF VIETNAM

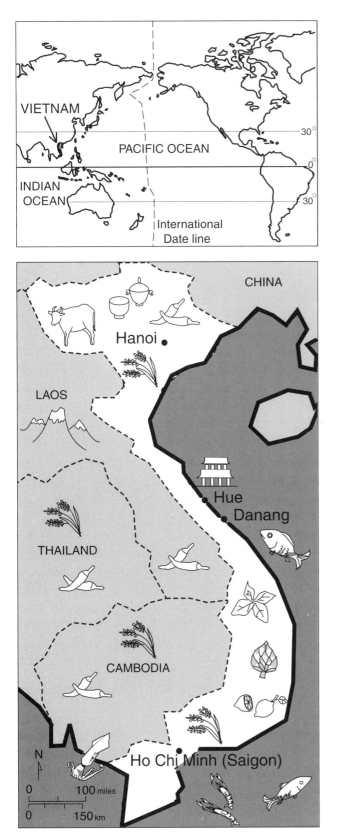

Vietnamese cuisine has been greatly influenced by two major factors. One is its own diverse microclimates that makes it hot and dry in one area, while another is experiencing monsoon weather. The second factor is the influence of its neighboring countries of China to the North, Laos, Cambodia, and Thailand to the West, and of course one should not overlook the significance of its "neighbor" to the East, the South China Sea. Therefore, each region has created its own unique style of cooking while continuing to use many of the exact same common ingredients.

Rice is the staple food of the entire country. Rice is not only used as a whole grain item, but also finely milled to produce flour to prepare other foods, and to make noodles. Rice or noodles are eaten at every meal including breakfast. Fish is another very important part of the diet. The long stretch of coastline lends a close proximity to a plentiful supply of fresh fish to many. Vegetables, herbs and spices are also key ingredients, and in abundant supply to enhance the Vietnamese dishes.

In the Northern Region nearest to China, stir-fried dishes are popular. In the Capital City of Hanoi, it is said they are the self-appointed preservers of "true Vietnamese" and their authentic dishes are prepared with a hint of foreign influence.

Hue was once Vietnam's Imperial City. It is known for *Banh Khoai*; a rice pancake filled with shrimp and pork, and *Bun Bo Hue*; a rice noodle dish. These two well-known dishes distinguish Hue along with the radial symmetry of Hue's Imperial food presentation.

Further south there is a strong French influence. For instance in Ho Chi Minh (formerly Saigon) rice, noodles, and sandwiches made with baguettes are popular. Overall, seafood is preferred over meat that is the preference in Northern Regions.

Throughout all regions the emphasis is always on serving fresh vegetables and/or fresh herbs as side dishes along with dipping sauces such as *Nuoc Cham*.

The Harmony of these elements creates a Vietnamese Cuisine that is "something special".

7

Most Vietnamese dishes are served with many fresh, uncooked vegetables
and herbs such as basil leaves, mint leaves, and lemon grass along
with lots of fresh lime juice with a variety of dipping sauces.

Vietnamese people share dishes family style,
allowing everyone to enjoy the same dish.
Sharing food is fundamental to the faith of culture.

Before you plan the menu, some special attention should be given
to the ingredients you choose.
It is best and ideal to choose very fresh ingredients.
Seasonal items are abundant in quantity. However, ingredients
that have been salted and cured, brined or dried in the sun,
also contribute subtle flavors to many dishes.

Consider the number of people you serve and whether you serve for a family,
festive occasion, luncheon, dinner, picnic, etc.

Plan your menu with meat, seafood, and vegetables.
Make each dish with different cooking method such
as grilling, steaming and stir-frying.
Note that some vegetables require blanching before quick stir-frying.

Presentation of food is also important.
Each ingredient has its own flavor, texture and color.
It is important to appeal to the eye as well as to the tongue.

Before You Start

1 Read recipes carefully and thoroughly.
2 Write down all of the ingredients you will need to buy.
3 Check all cooking equipment and place within reach.
4 Arrange all necessary seasonings on your kitchen counter, or within your reach.
5 Place measuring cups and spoons to be ready for use.
6 Place all serving bowls, plates and platters within reach. You may need to keep some serving platters warm.
7 Prepare plenty of kitchen towels and paper towels.
8 Keep in mind that hot food should be served on a warmed plate and cold food on a chilled plate. Also, check the design on the plate before you place food on it. Place the plate so that the design faces the diner. Wipe the rims of all plates to remove any spilled bits or traces of liquid.

INGREDIENTS

For more information, check the glossary on page 90 - 93.

Fish sauce	Fish sauce (anchovy)	Oyster sauce	Hoisin sauce	Soy sauce	Light soy sauce	Vegetarian soy sauce	Japanese vinegar

Chili sauce	Chili paste	Salted soy beans	Bean sauce	Fine shrimp sauce	Crab paste	Sesame oil	Vegetable oil

Pickled lotus rootlets	Tamarind	Lotus seeds	Lychee	Coconut milk	Coconut juice	Coconut soda	*Tofu* sheets

Rice paper	Rice noodle (*Pho*)	Rice vermicelli	Egg noodles	*Saifun* noodles	Wood ear mushrooms

Jicama	Taro root	Eggplant	Sweet potato	*Kabocha* squash	Long beans

Bok choy	Basil	Lemon grass	Ginger	*Shiitake* mushrooms	Oyster mushroms

VEGETABLE SPRING ROLLS (Chả giò chay)

A colorful tray of appetizers is a good way to start the evening.

Ingredients (makes 8)
Filling:
  4 oz (120 g) *tofu* (bean curd), drained
  1 cup each, shredded carrot, jicama
  1 cup chopped celery
  ½ cup shredded taro roots
  ½ cup chopped onion
  ¼ cup softened wood ear
    mushroom shreds
  ¼ cup softened *saifun* noodles
  2 tsp chopped garlic
  ½ tsp each, salt and pepper

8 sheets rice paper, 8½" (22 cm) in
  diameter
Oil for deep-frying
Nuoc Cham Dipping Sauce (page 88)

10

① Soak the wood ear mushrooms and noodles in water until soft about 15 minutes; drain.

② Finely chopped vegetables: jicama, taro root, carrot, celery, onion, and garlic.

③ In a bowl, combine the vegetables and squeezed tofu. Season to taste with salt and pepper. Squeeze tofu and vegetables to remove excess liquid.

④ Add mushrooms and noodles to the bowl and stir well.

⑤ In lukewarm water, dip the rice paper to moisten, one sheet at a time.

⑥ Lay a sheet of rice paper, and spread one-eighth of the filling evenly.

⑦ Fold up bottom end and then sides to wrap the filling.

⑧ Roll up firmly, and place the rolls seam sides down until frying.

⑨ Deep-fry at 350°F (180°C) until golden and crisp. Serve with *Nuoc Cham* Dipping Sauce.

FISH SPRING ROLLS (Chả giò cá)

Ingredients (makes 8)

Filling:
  6 oz (180 g) white fish fillets, ground
  1 cup diced onion
  ¼ cup chopped green onion
  2 Tbsp chopped lemon grass
  1 Tbsp chopped peanuts
  1 tsp each, salt and pepper
  1 tsp chopped garlic
  1 tsp sugar
8 sheets rice paper, 8½" (22 cm) in
  diameter
Oil for deep-frying
Bean Dipping Sauce (page 88)

Everyone's favorite, white meat fish makes for a great spring roll filling.

① Prepare all filling ingredients.

② In a bowl, combine all ingredients, and season with salt, pepper and sugar.

③ Wet rice paper, one by one.

④ Divide the filling into 8, and place a single portion on a softened rice paper sheet. Fold up bottom end, then sides to wrap the filling. Roll up firmly, and place the rolls seam sides down.

⑤ Deep-fry at 350°F (180°C) until lightly browned. Serve with Bean Dipping Sauce.

Rice Paper

Rice paper is made from ground rice flour, and comes in various sizes (6"/15 cm, 8½"/22 cm, 12¼"/31 cm etc). It should be soaked in water to soften before use.

GOLDEN PORK SPRING ROLLS (Chả giò /Nem rán)

One of the most popular dishes at Andre's restaurant.

Ingredients (makes 8)
Filling:
   8 oz (240 g) ground pork
   1 cup each, shredded jicama and carrots
   ¼ cup diced onion
   ¼ cup softened *saifun* noodles
   ¼ cup softened wood ear mushroom shreds
   ½ tsp each, sugar, salt and pepper
8 sheets rice paper or egg roll wrappers, softened
   (8½"/22 cm in diameter)
Oil for deep-frying
Nuoc Cham Dipping Sauce (page 88)

① Soak *saifaun* noodles and wood ear mushrooms until soft for at least 15 minutes.

② Cut carrots, jicama, and onion; squeeze well.

③ In a bowl, combine all ingredients for filling.

④ Lay a rice paper sheet, and spread one-eighth of the filling. Wrap and roll firmly. Deep-fry at 350℉ (180℃) until golden and crisp. Serve with *Nuoc Cham* Dipping Sauce.

FRESH SPRING ROLLS (Gỏi cuốn)

A see-through, delicious salad roll dish that fits perfectly in a grand party menu.

Ingredients (makes 4)
Filling:
   4 oz (120 g) pork loin
   8 medium shrimp
   2 oz (60 g) rice vermicelli
   4 lettuce leaves
   1 cup bean sprouts
   16 - 20 fresh mint leaves
   8 pieces garlic chives
4 sheets rice paper, 12¼"(31 cm) in diameter
1 Tbsp coconut milk
Bean Dipping Sauce (page 88)

① Cook pork in boiling water until done; drain and slice thinly. Cook shrimp in boiling water until done; drain and shell.

② Soak rice vermicelli in water until soft for 15 minutes and drain.

③ Soften rice paper in lukewarm water, one sheet at a time, and lay on a flat surface. Place vegetables and rice vermicelli near to you. Then pork and shrimp, and lastly garlic chives.

④ Roll up. Serve with Bean Dipping Sauce.

SHRIMP SPRING ROLLS (Chả giò tôm)

Crisp on the outside, soft and moist inside.

Ingredients (makes 8)

Filling:
    8 medium size shrimp, shelled and deveined
    8-10 shallots, cut into quarters
    1 small knob ginger, finely shredded
    ½ tsp salt
    ½ tsp sugar
    Dash pepper
8 sheets rice paper, 8½"(22 cm) in diameter
1½ tsp turmeric, dissolved in 1 qt(4 cups) water
Oil for deep-frying

① In a large bowl, mix all ingredients.

② Lay a sheet of rice paper, and brush surface with turmeric water.

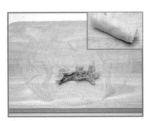

③ Place one-eighth of the filling on rice paper, near to you. Fold near end of rice paper over filling, then overlap the sides. Roll up.

④ Deep-fry in hot oil of about 350℉(180℃) until golden brown. Serve while hot, accompanied with *Nuoc Cham* Vinaigrette (page 88) and lettuce leaves to wrap up, if you prefer.

SOFT CREPE SPRING ROLLS (Bánh cuốn tôm thịt)

Ingredients (makes 16)
Filling:
   3 oz (100 g) ground pork
   2 oz (60 g) shrimp, chopped
   ½ cup softened wood ear mushroom
      shreds
   ½ cup chopped onion
   2 tsp fish sauce
   2 tsp sugar
   ⅛ tsp each, salt and pepper
   1 Tbsp oil for stir-frying
Wrappers:
   6 oz (170 g) *Bot Do Banh Cuon*
      flour mix
2 cups water

Serve as an appetizer or as a side dish.

① Chop softened wood ear mushrooms as well as other ingredients.

② Heat oil in a wok; sauté onion and ground pork. Add chopped shrimp and pork and mushrooms. Season with fish sauce, sugar, salt and pepper. Stir-fry for 2-3 minutes. Set aside to cool.

③ In a bowl, combine flour and water. Let stand for a few minutes.

④ Spray oil lightly over a non-stick pan. Pour in about 4 Tbsp flour mixture evenly, and cook until set, to make a thin "crepe". Make 16.

⑤ Divide the cooled filling into 16, and place a single portion on a crepe. Fold both sides in and roll up into a rectangle. Serve with *Nuoc Cham* Dipping Sauce.

Bot Do Banh Cuon Flour Mix

A pre-mixed flour for making crepe, sold in Asian food markets. It can be substituted with rice flour and tapoica starch in the ratio of 6:1.

BROILED LEMON GRASS PRAWNS (Tôm nướng xả)

Ideal for an intimate party.

Ingredients (makes 4)
12 prawns, shelled and deveined
Marinade Sauce:
   2 Tbsp chopped lemon grass
   1 Tbsp olive oil
   1 Tbsp honey
   1 Tbsp fish sauce
   2 tsp curry powder
   2 green onion, finely chopped
1 tsp chili paste
4 stalks lemon grass
Tamarind Dipping Sauce (page 88)

① Combine all Marinade Sauce ingredients, and marinate prawns for 15 minutes.

② Cut lemon grass into 10"(25 cm) lengths. "Skewer" prawns with lemon grass. Grill or broil prawns and serve with Tamarind Dipping Sauce.

Lemom Grass

A tall, strong, and graceful grass found in warm climates. The plant has a tough fibrous stem which releases a very delicate refreshing aroma resembling that of a lemon.

SHRIMP PASTE WRAPPED AROUND SUGER CANE (Chạo tôm)

Ingredients (makes 4)
10 oz (300 g) baby shrimp
1 Tbsp chopped onion
1 Tbsp sliced green onion
2 tsp chopped garlic
1 Tbsp vegetable oil
Seasoning:
  1 Tbsp fish sauce
  2 tsp each, mayonnaise, and
    paprika powder
  2 tsp beaten egg white
  1 tsp each, corn starch, baking
    powder, and sugar
  1/2 tsp white pepper
  1/8 tsp salt
8 pieces sugar cane in syrup
Nuoc Cham Dipping Sauce (page 88)

Sugar cane adds a festive touch.

① Clean and shell shrimp. Wipe off moisture well.

② Chop shrimp well until smooth.

③ Heat 1 Tbsp oil, sauté chopped onion, green onion and garlic. When cooled, combine with chopped shrimp and all Seasoning ingredients.

④ Wrap one-eighth of shrimp mixture around a 4"(10 cm) piece of sugar cane.

⑤ In a preheated steamer, steam for 10-15 minutes until done. Charbroil just before serving, and accompany with *Nuoc Cham* Dipping Sauce.

Sugar Cane

Sugar cane is available canned and sometimes fresh, and its outer skin should be peeled before use.

GOLDEN SHRIMP CAKE (Tàu hũ ky bọc tôm)

An attractive dish that uses *tofu* sheets as wrappers.

Ingredients (makes 4)
10 oz (300 g) baby shrimp
1 Tbsp chopped onions
1 Tbsp sliced green onion
2 tsp chopped garlic
1 Tbsp vegetable oil
Seasoning:
  1 Tbsp fish sauce
  2 tsp each, mayonnaise, paprika powder
  2 tsp egg white, beaten
  1 tsp each, cornstarch, baking powder, sugar
  ½ tsp white pepper
  ⅛ tsp salt

1 large frozen *tofu* sheet, thawed
Oil for deep-frying
Nuoc Cham Dipping Sauce (page 88)

① Prepare shrimp paste referring to Steps 1-3 on page 18 (Makes about 2 cups).

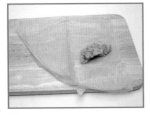

② Cut *tofu* sheet into quarters or 12"(30 cm) squares. Place ½ cup of the shrimp paste on a sheet.

③ Fold up ends to resemble a parcel. Seal the edges with beaten egg white. Deep-fry in 350℉ (180℃) oil until golden. Serve with *Nuoc Cham* Dipping Sauce.

***Tofu* Sheets**

Thin films formed in *tofu*-making process. *Tofu* sheets come in folded and frozen form so that you can cut to the desired size before use.

CRISPY CALAMARI (Mực chiên dòn)

A simple way to make an ideal snack.

Beer Batter

Ingredients (serves 4)
6 oz (180 g) squid
  1 cup all purpose flour
Beer Batter:
  1 cup each, all purpose flour and cornstarch
  4 Tbsp rice flour
  2 tsp sugar
  1 tsp each, baking soda and baking powder
  1 tsp each, paprika, turmeric powder, and salt
  1 cup each, water and fresh beer
Oil for deep-frying
Chili plum sauce

Chili Plum Sauce

A sauce made from plums and apricots as well as vinegar, sugar and chili pepper.

① Mix all dry ingredients for Beer Batter, then add water and beer, and whisk well. Set aside at room temperature for 2-3 hours before using.

② Cut squid into strips of a pencil size. Blanch in boiling water; drain.

③ Dust squid strips with flour.

④ Heat oil to 350°F - 375°F (180°C -190°C). Dip squid strips into Beer Batter, and deep-fry until golden brown. Serve with chili plum sauce.

BROILED PETIT OCTOPUS (Mực non nướng)

The key ingredient is, surprisingly, corn syrup.

Ingredients (serves 4)
1 lb (450 g) small octopus
Marinade Sauce:
  ½ cup chopped green onion
  1 Tbsp fish sauce
  1 Tbsp vegetable oil
  1 Tbsp corn syrup
  2 tsp chili flakes
  2 tsp chopped garlic
  ½ tsp curry powder
Tamarind Dipping Sauce (page 88)

① Cut octopus head in half and clean inside, removing brown "beaks".

② Combine all Marinade Sauce ingredients and marinate octopus for 1-2 hours.

③ Skewer octopus pieces and broil until done. Serve hot, accompanied with Tamarind Dipping Sauce.

GRILLED CHINESE EGGPLANTS (Cà tìm nướng)

Serve with hot rice for a great vegetarian meal.

Ingredients (serves 4)
2 Chinese eggplants
Sauce:
  ½ cup coconut milk
  ½ cup chopped green onion
  1 Tbsp fish sauce or soy sauce
  1 tsp sugar
  1 tsp olive oil
  ½ tsp chopped garlic

① Grill eggplants until browned all around, and soft inside.

② Peel off skin while hot, and trim away cap.

③ Slice diagonally into bite-size pieces, and arrange on a serving plate.

④ Heat all Sauce ingredients to a boil, and pour over eggplant pieces.

POTATO FRITTERS (Bánh khoai cổ ngư)

A unique combination of potato and shrimp.

Ingredients (serves 4-6)
2 lbs (900 g) yam
6 oz (170 g) small shrimp
1 carrot
Salt and pepper
Beer Batter (page 20)
Nuoc Cham Dipping Sauce (page 88)
Oil for deep-frying

① Make Beer Batter referring to page 20. Peel and cut yam and carrot into strips of 2½" (7 cm) length and ⅜" (1 cm) width.

② Mix yam, carrot and shrimp. Coat the mixture with Beer Batter.

③ Deep-fry until the batter becomes crisp. Drain and serve with *Nuoc Cham* Dipping Sauce.

TARO ROOT BISQUE (Canh khoai)

An easy side dish, or a complete meal.

Ingredients (serves 4-6)
6 cups chicken or pork stock (page 89)
  3 Tbsp fish sauce
  1 Tbsp sugar
1 lb (450 g) taro root, shredded (about 6 cups)
4-6 medium size shrimp, shelled
  1 green onion, chopped (about 2 Tbsp)
  1 tsp fish sauce
  ½ tsp sugar
Garnish:
  Fresh cumin leaves, cilantro, basil

① In a soup pot, put stock, sugar and fish sauce. Bring to a boil.

② Add taro to the pot and simmer for 25 minutes. Skim any bubbles that float.

③ Using a side of a wide knife, flatten shrimp on a cutting board.

④ Combine flattened shrimp, chopped green onion, fish sauce and sugar. Add this mixture to the pot. Simmer for a few minutes. Serve garnished with cumin, cilantro, and basil leaves.

STUFFED CABBAGE ROLL SOUP (Canh bắp cải nhồi thịt)

Ingredients (serves 4)
6 cups chicken or pork stock (page 89)
　1 Tbsp dried shrimp
　2 tsp fish sauce
　1 tsp sugar
4 large cabbage leaves
　6 cups water
　1 tsp salt
Stuffing:
　6 oz (180 g) lean ground pork
　2 oz (60 g) shrimp, shelled
　1-2 green onion
　¼ cup softened *saifun* noodles ,optional
　2 *shiitake* mushrooms
　1 Tbsp softened wood ear mushroom shreds
　1 tsp each, fish sauce and sugar
4 green onions for tying

A soup dish of colorful fillings rolled in cabbage leaves.

① Make shrimp stock by cooking the dried shrimp, fish sauce and sugar in 6 cups of chicken or pork stock for 15 minutes; discard the shrimp.

② Cook cabbage leaves in lightly salted water until soft. Trim away hard stems; set aside. Chop green onion, softened wood ear mushrooms and *saifun* noodles. Slice *shiitake* mushrooms.

③ Combine chopped onion and mushrooms with ground pork and shrimp.

④ Place one-fourth of the stuffing at the stem end of each leaf, and fold in the sides.

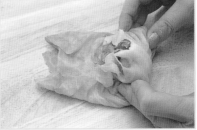

⑤ Roll each leaf tightly. Cook green onions briefly and tie around each roll.

⑥ Cook rolls in the stock for 20 minutes until fork-tender.

25

ASPARAGUS AND CORN SOUP (Canh măng tây & bắp)

Add a new dimension to your favorite repertoire.

Ingredients (serves 4)
6 cups vegetable broth
6 oz (170 g) fresh white asparagus
  (use only tender parts)
8 oz (230 g) frozen or canned corn
3 oz (90 g) crab meat with juice
2 tsp sugar
1 tsp soy sauce
2 tsp salt

Thickener:
  5 Tbsp cornstarch dissolved in 5
  Tbsp water
1 egg, beaten
2 tsp sesame oil
Garnish:
  1 Tbsp chopped green onion
  1 Tbsp chopped cilantro

① Cut asparagus into 1½"(4 cm) lengths. Discard hard ends.

② Bring the vegetable broth to a boil. Add soy sauce, sugar and salt. Swirl in the dissolved cornstarch to thicken broth.

③ Add crab meat, asparagus and corn.

④ Swirl in beaten egg slowly and sesame oil, stir well. Serve garnished with green onion and cilantro.

TAMARIND SOUP (Canh chua me)

Ingredients (serves 4-6)
5 cups shrimp or fish stock (page 89)
   2 oz (60 g) sugar
   4 Tbsp fish sauce
   1 Tbsp tamarind powder
   1 Tbsp sour shrimp paste
    or *Tom Yam* paste
6 oz (170 g) white fish fillets
   such as catfish, cod or halibut
1 cup sliced pineapple
4 fresh okra pods
1 tomato, wedged
2 cups bean sprouts
2 cups sliced fresh taro stem
Garnish:
   Fresh mint leaves, shredded
   Chili peppers, sliced

An ideal, refreshing summer-time treat.

① Cut fish fillets into serving pieces.

② Slice okra and taro stems diagonally. Cut drained pineapple into chunks.

③ In a large pot, place the stock and seasonings. Stir and bring to a boil. Add the fish pieces and cook for 3 minutes over medium heat.

④ Add all vegetables except for mint leaves and chili.

⑤ Continue to cook for 5 minutes. Serve hot garnished with mint leaves and chili.

Sour Shrimp Paste

Thick paste made from shrimp, garlic, sugar, vinegar and chili pepper. It is used as a base for spicy pot dishes or soups.

KIEM VEGETARIAN SOUP (Canh kiểm)

The savory ingredients enrich this dish.

Ingredients (serves 4)
½ cup raw peanuts
½ *kabocha* squash
6 oz (180 g) sweet potato
½ carrot
2 oz (60 g) long beans
1 cake deep-fried *tofu*, diced
6 cups water
1 cup coconut milk
3 Kaffir lime leaves
2 tsp curry paste
1 Tbsp chopped ginger
3 oz (90 g) bamboo shoot strips

2 cups canned creamed corn
1 Tbsp salt

① Cook raw peanuts in salted, boiling water for 10 minutes.

② Cut vegetables; sweet potato, carrot, *kabocha* squash into chunks, and long beans into 1½" (4 cm) lengths.

③ Cut fried *tofu* into bite-size pieces.

④ In a medium saucepan, pour 6 cups of water and bring to a boil. Add all vegetables and cook over medium heat for about 15-20 minutes.

⑤ Add coconut milk, Kaffir lime leaves, curry paste, ginger, peanuts and *tofu*.

⑥ Add bamboo shoots, creamed corn, salt. Cook for another 10 minutes.

GREEN PAPAYA SALAD (Gỏi đu đủ)

Nuoc Cham Vinaigrette is the secret ingredient.

Ingredients (serves 4)

1 green papaya
1 carrot
6 oz (170 g) lean pork or white chicken meat
8 medium size shrimp, shelled and deveined
1 Tbsp store-bought fried shallots
2 Tbsp store-bought diced roasted peanuts
5-6 mint leaves
Nuoc Cham Vinaigrette:
   ½ cup each, *Nuoc Cham* Dipping Sauce (page 88), sugar, and water
   ¼ cup each, lime juice and Japanese rice vinegar
   2 Tbsp chopped garlic
   2 tsp chili paste

③ Combine all ingredients for *Nuoc Cham* Vinaigrette.

④ On a serving dish, mound shredded vegetables, and arrange shrimp and pork or ckicken on top. Garnish with shredded mint leave and sprinkle with shallots and peanuts. Serve with *Nuoc Cham* Vinaigrette.

① Shred green papaya and carrot finely.

② Cook shrimp briefly in lightly salted, boiling water, and drain. Cook pork or chicken by boiling or steaming; drain and let stand to cool. Shred mint leaves.

CHICKEN SALAD (Gỏi gà)

Sure to be one of your favorites for everyday meals.

Ingredients (serves 4)
1 head green cabbage
1 head red cabbage
1 carrot
3 oz (90 g) skinless white chicken
1 red onion
2-3 mint leaves
2 Tbsp Japanese rice vinegar
½ tsp salt
1 Tbsp store-bought roasted shallots
2 Tbsp store-bought diced roasted peanuts
Nuoc Cham Vinaigrette (page 88)

① Prepare vegetables: shred cabbages, carrot and mint leaves. Slice red onion.

② Cook chicken in boiling water; drain and slice. In a large bowl, toss all vegetables and cooled chicken slices.

③ Sprinkle with shallots and peanuts, if desired. Serve with basil leaves, lime wedge and *Nuoc Cham* Vinaigrette to pour over salad.

LOTUS ROOT SALAD (Gỏi ngó sen)

Lotus roots turn into a legendary Vietnamese delicacy.

Ingredients (serves 4)
1 lb (450 g) pickled lotus rootlets
1 cucumber
½ red bell pepper
½ each, carrot and red onion
12 medium size shrimp, shelled
2 oz (60 g) lean pork or chicken
2 tsp sugar
1 tsp salt
2-3 mint leaves, shredded
1 Tbsp store-bought diced roasted peanuts
Nuoc Cham Vinaigrette (page 88)

① Cut all vegetables into fine shreds.

② Cook pork or chicken and slice thinly. Cook shrimp.

③ Toss all vegetables with sugar and salt. Sprinkle with lime juice, if you prefer.

④ Mound vegetables and arrange sliced pork and shrimp on top. Sprinkle with roasted peanuts and shredded mint leaves. Serve with *Nuoc Cham* Vinaigrette.

WARM ASIAN SPINACH SALAD (Gỏi rau muống)

This unique curly stem of Asian spinach can be eaten fresh or stir-fried.

Ingredients (makes 4)
2 lbs (900 g) Asian spinach
  1 tsp lemon juice
  ½ tsp salt
1 tomato
½ red onion
12 oz (340 g) flank steak beef
Marinade Sauce:
  1 Tbsp soy sauce
  1 Tbsp chopped garlic
  3 tsp sugar
  ½ tsp pepper

3 Tbsp oil for stir-frying
4" (10 cm) piece green onion
Store-bought roasted shallots, optional
Store-bought diced roasted peanuts, optional
Nuoc Cham Vinaigrette (page 88)

① Remove leaves from Asian spinach, and cut the stems into thin, thread-like shreds. Toss in water in lemon juice and salt.

② Slice red onion. Cut tomato into wedges. Slice beef thinly.

③ Combine all Marinade Sauce ingredients and marinate beef in the mixture. Heat a wok and add oil. Brown beef slices and add red onion.

④ Arrange beef slices and tomato on top. Pour over *Nuoc Cham* Vinaigrette or any dressing of your choice. Sprinkle with the roasted shallots and peanuts.

FISH SEVICHE SALAD (Gỏi cá tươi)

Lime juice and coconut soda bring out the distinctive flavor.

Ingredients (serves 4)

1 lb (450 g) very fresh fish fillets
Marinade Sauce:
   3 limes or 6 Tbsp lime juice
   ³/₄ tsp salt
   3 Tbsp Japanese rice vinegar
1 red onion
1 green onion
½ red bell pepper
4-5 mint leaves

Srimp Dipping Sauce (makes 2 cups):
   ½ cup sour shrimp paste
   ½ cup sugar
   ½ cup lime juice
   ½ cup coconut soda
   1 Tbsp chili paste
   2 Tbsp chopped garlic
Store-bought roasted shallots,optional
Store-bought diced roasted peanuts,optional
Fried shrimp rice crackers, optional

① Slice fish fillets very thinly. Cut limes halves and squeeze out.

② In a bowl, place fish slices. Combine with lime juice, rice vinegar and salt. Marinate fish in this vinegar mixture for 10-15 minutes.

③ Slice red and green onions, bell pepper, and mint leaves. Toss all and mound on a serving plate. Arrange marinated fish slices. Sprinkle with shallots and peanuts. Serve with Shrimp Dipping Sauce.

SCAMPI IN COCONUT JUICE (Tôm càng rim dừa tươi)

Coconut juice adds a delicate flavor.

Ingredients (makes 4)
4 scampi or large prawns
¼ onion
1 green onion
1"(25 cm) square ginger
2 Tbsp olive oil for stir-frying
Seasoning:
  1½ cups coconut juice
  2 Tbsp fish sauce
  1 Tbsp tomato paste or tomato ketchup
  1 Tbsp Maggie Seasoning or Viet-
    namese soy sauce

1 Tbsp sugar
1 tsp chili flakes
½ tsp freshly ground black pepper
Garnish:
  Cilantro

① Slice onion into thick pieces. Cut green onion and ginger.

② Clean prawns or scampi, and trim away tips of heads.

③ In a heated wok, stir-fry onion, ginger, green onion. Add prawns and cook for 2-3 minutes.

④ Add all Seasoning ingredients to the wok, and stir well. Garnish with cilantro leaves. Serve with steamed rice, if you prefer.

DUNGENESS CRAB FARCI (Cua nhồi)

An attractive dish for entertaining guests.

Ingredients (serves 4)
2-3 lbs(900-1350 g) whole crab, cooked
10 Thai basil leaves
Stuffing:
  1 cup crabmeat taken from crab
    above
  ½ cup softened *saifun* noodles
  1 egg, beaten
  2 *shiitake* mushrooms
  ¼ onion, diced
  1 Tbsp cornstarch

1 Tbsp fish sauce
1 tsp sugar
½ tsp chopped garlic
Salt and pepper
1 egg yolk

① Scoop out crabmeat and save top shell. Lay basil leaves on the bottom.

② Combine stuffing ingredients well, and fill the lined shell.

③ In an oven preheated to 350°F (180°C), bake for 15 minutes. Take out and brush egg yolk over the surface, and continue to bake another 10 minutes.

MOM'S FISH IN CLAY POT (Cà kho tộ)

Excellent served with steamed jasmine rice.

Ingredients (makes 2-4)
16 - 18oz (450-500 g) fish fillet with skin,
　such as catfish, red snapper, cod or halibut
4 green onions, cut into 1½"(4 cm) lengths
½ oz (15 g) ginger, sliced
4-5 cloves garlic, crushed
¼ cup fish sauce
¼ cup sugar
2 tsp chili flakes
Dash of pepper
1 Tbsp store-bought syrup
1 Tbsp oil for stir-frying

① Cut fish fillet into serving size. Heat 1 Tbsp oil in a pan, and fry garlic and ginger. Add green onion.

② Add fish pieces and brown on both sides.

③ Add fish sauce, sugar, chili flakes and pepper.

④ Transfer to a clay pot. Add syrup, and simmer covered for 15-20 minutes.

CRISPY WHOLE FISH (Cá chiên xù)

Crisp outside, moist inside, and deep-fried without being greasy.

Dipping Sauce

Ingredients (serves 4)
2 lbs (900 g) whole fish such as
   red snapper, catfish, striped bass
2 egg whites
Cornstarch for coating
Salt and pepper
Oil for deep-frying

Dipping Sauce:
   4 green onions
   ½ red bell pepper
   ½ cup chili sauce for chicken
   2 Tbsp fish sauce
   2 Tbsp lime juice (squeezed from
      1 lime)
   2 tsp sugar
   2 Tbsp oil for stir-frying

① Clean fish, inside and outside.

② Sprinkle fish with salt and pepper.

③ Coat with lightly beaten egg whites.

④ Dust with cornstarch on both sides. In hot oil at 375°F(190°C), deep-fry fish until done, turning once.

⑤ Make Dipping Sauce: Chop red bell pepper and green onions. In a skillet, heat 2 Tbsp oil and stir-fry them.

⑥ Add lime juice, chili sauce, fish sauce and sugar. Stir well. Arrange fried fish with sliced onions, carrot flowers and cilantro. Serve with Dipping Sauce.

CHICKEN WITH MUSHROOMS (Gà xào nấm)

A delicious Vietnamese version of stir-fried chicken.

Cooking Sauce

Ingredients (serves 4)

10 oz (300 g) skinless, boneless
   chicken breast
  2 Tbsp cornstarch
  1 Tbsp vegetable oil
  2 tsp salt
  8 *shiitake* mushrooms
  8 oyster mushrooms
  8 button mushrooms
  ½ red onion
  4 oz (120 g) sugar pea pods
  ½ red bell pepper

Cooking Sauce:
  2 Tbsp Vietnamese soy sauce
  1 Tbsp fish sauce
  2 tsp sugar
  1 cup chicken stock
  1 tsp chopped garlic
16 Thai basil leaves
Thickener:
  1 Tbsp cornstarch dissolved with
    2 Tbsp water
Oil for stir-frying

① Cut chicken into long strips and sprinkle with salt, oil and cornstarch; let stand for 10 minutes. In a wok, heat 1 Tbsp oil and sauté chicken until lightly browned; remove chicken.

② Add 1 Tbsp oil and stir-fry sliced mushrooms, onion and pepper over medium high heat.

③ Add chicken pieces, Cooking Sauce ingredients and basil leaves. Cook and stir for a minute and quickly swirl in thickener .

44

STEAMED CHICKEN AND MUSTARD GREEN (Gà hấp cải xanh)

Best when served with hot steamed rice.

Ingredients (serves 4)

10-12 oz (300-360 g) boneless,
  skinless chicken breast
8 oz (230 g) Chinese mustard greens
¼ carrot, thinly sliced
1 Tbsp shredded ginger

Cooking Sauce:
  1 Tbsp soy sauce
  1 Tbsp oyster sauce
  1 tsp sugar
  ¼ tsp sesame oil
  1 cup chicken stock
Thickener:
  1 Tbsp cornstarch dissolved in
    2 Tbsp water

① Cook chicken breast in boiling water until done; remove chicken and let cool. Save stock.

② Cut mustard greens lengthwise in half, and blanch in boiling water together with carrot; drain.

③ Line a bowl with greens, then fill with chicken pieces. Place half amount of carrot slices. In a preheated steamer, cook for 20-30 minutes.

④ Transfer onto a serving plate by turning over bowl, and garnish with rest of carrot slices. In a saucepan, heat Cooking Sauce ingredients to a boil. Quickly swirl in thickener, and pour over chicken. Decorate with carrot flowers for a color effect.

45

LEMON GRASS CHICKEN (Gà xào xả ớt)

Ingredients (serves 4)
10 oz (285 g) chicken meat,
    cut into bite-size pieces
  2 Tbsp cornstarch
  1 Tbsp vegetable oil
  2 tsp salt
Cooking Sauce:
  2 Tbsp chopped lemon grass
  1 Tbsp Vietnamese soy sauce or
    teriyaki sauce
  ½ Tbsp each, fish sauce and sugar
  1 tsp chili flakes
  1 tsp chopped garlic
  2 dried chili peppers
½ red onion, diced
16-20 Thai basil leaves
¼ cup coconut juice

Goes very well with either hot rice or noodles.

① Sprinkle chicken with salt and cornstarch.

② Combine Cooking Sauce ingredients in a small bowl.

③ Heat oil in a wok, and saute chicken over medium high heat, until lightly browned.

④ Add Cooking Sauce. Cook and stir for a minute.

⑤ Stir in onion, basil, and coconut juice. Cook about 1 minute.

Thai Basil

Most basil you find in Asian market is Thai basil. It has shiny green leaves, and sometimes, purple stems. It tastes different from European varieties of basil, and is best to use fresh.

CHICKEN WITH COCONUT JUICE (Gà hầm với dừa tươi)

The chicken develops in irresistibly hearty flavor when slow simmered.

Ingredients (serves 4)
1 whole chicken or 4 chicken breasts
Cooking Sauce:
   1 cup diced onion
   1 Tbsp each, soy sauce and chopped garlic
   2 Tbsp Maggie Seasoning
   2 tsp each, salt and sugar
   1 tsp black pepper
½ cup dry or sweet sherry wine
1 cup (8 oz / 236 ml) coconut juice
3 Tbsp olive oil

① Cut up whole chicken into about 12 pieces.

② Sauté chicken in 3 Tbsp oil until lightly browned.

③ Add Cooking Sauce ingredients, and simmer covered for 10 minutes, skimming scums.

④ Pour in sherry wine and coconut juice, and simmer for another 20 minutes.

STUFFED GAME HEN (Gà nhỏ nhồi thịt)

Appropriate for festive occasions.

Ingredients (serves 4)

1 whole game hen, cleaned

Stuffing:

  8 oz (230 g) ground pork, chicken, or turkey

  ½ cup coarsely chopped cashew nuts

  ¼ cup each, diced onion, carrot, and jicama

  ¼ cup softened wood ear mushroom shreds

  2 tsp Maggi Seasoning

  1 tsp salt

  Pinch pepper

1 Tbsp oil for brushing

① Preheat oven. Bone hen, placing breast side down. Using a boning knife, cut along center of back and open flat. Remove bones.

② Cut off tip of each wing, using a cleaver.

③ Combine all stuffing ingredients.

④ Spread stuffing over open game hen.

⑤ Pull sides together to close opening.

⑥ Truss up hen with care as shown, using bamboo skewers to "weave" skin. Place in a baking dish and roast in 350 ℉(180℃) oven for 30-35 minutes, occasionally brushing with oil.

BRAISED DUCK WITH ORANGE (Vịt hầm với cam)

Fresh tangerine oranges make this dish outstandingly tasty.

Ingredients (serves 4)
1 (4-5 lbs/1800-2250 g) whole duck
   1 tsp salt
   ½ tsp pepper
1 onion, chopped
Orange Sauce:
   2 cups chicken stock
   ½ cup each, ketchup, and orange liqueur
   1 cup juice tangerine
   4 Tbsp fish sauce
   2 Tbsp honey
   ½ tsp chili sauce
3 Tbsp oil for stir-frying

① Clean and cut duck into 20 pieces. Sprinkle with salt and pepper; set a side.

② Heat oil in a heavy skillet. Sauté duck until slightly browned. Discard excess grease.

③ Add chopped onion and Orange Sauce ingredients; simmer covered for 30-40 minutes, occasionally skimming froth.

SEVEN SPICE BEEF (Bò thất vị)

A variety of spices give the beef a rich flavor.

Ingredients (serves 4)

1 lb (450 g) tenderloin, flank or top sirloin beef

Marinade Sauce:
  3 Tbsp hoisin sauce
  1 Tbsp each, sugar and honey
  1 tsp each, sesame oil and oyster sauce
  1 tsp each, cumin powder, black pepper, five-spice powder, nutmeg, coriander, and chili powder

1 lb (450 g) baby bok choy

1 green onion, cut into 1"(2.5 cm) length

1/4 red or yellow bell pepper, cut into 1"(2.5 cm) squares

1/4 red onion, cut up

1 tsp oil for stir-frying

① Slice meat into 1/8" (3 mm) thickness.

② Combine all Marinade Sauce ingredients and marinate beef slices for 15 minutes.

③ Cook bok choy in boiling water, drain and place on a serving platter.

④ Heat oil in wok, and stir-fry beef halfway done; set aside. Stir-fry green onion, pepper and onion briefly, then put back beef. Place over bok choy.

BROILED BEEF ROLLS (Bò nướng kim tiền)

Ingredients (serves 4)
1 lb (450 g) flank steak
Marinade Sauce:
  3 Tbsp soy sauce
  2 tsp vegetable oil
  2 tsp sugar
  Pinch black pepper
Stuffing:
  2 Tbsp chopped shallots
  2 Tbsp chopped green onion
  2 *shiitake* mushrooms, sliced
  12-15 Thai basil leaves, chopped
  1 tsp oil for stir-fring

Marinated and broiled beef enhanced with Thai basil.

① Using a mallet, flatten flank steak, and cut in half. Sprinkle Marinade Sauce over them and set aside.

② Prepare stuffing ingredients, and fry them in 1 tsp oil. Let stand to cool.

③ Spread cooled stuffing over center of beef.

④ Roll up tightly, and secure with string.

⑤ Place rolls between double grilling grid, and BBQ or grill as desired. (Or heat oil in a skillet and pan-fry rolled beef until lightly browned. Cover and cook over minimum heat until done).

⑥ Remove string and slice into 1"(2.5 cm) thick slices.

BROILED BEEF WITH LEMON GRASS (Bò nướng xả)

Lemon grass adds the flavor to beef.

Ingredients (serves 4)

½ lb (230 g) top round or flank
   steak beef, thinly sliced

Marinade Sauce:

   ¼ onion
   2 cloves garlic
   10 curry leaves, chopped
   4 Tbsp coconut milk
   2 Tbsp each, fish sauce and chopped lemon grass
   1 Tbsp sugar
   2 tsp each, curry powder, curry paste, chili flakes
   1 tsp vegetable oil

½ onion, sliced
½ red bell pepper, sliced

① Prepare Marinade Sauce by chopping lemon grass, garlic, curry leaves and onion.

② Combine all Marinade ingredients. Cut beef into chunks and marinate. Let stand for an hour: drain.

③ Using 6" (20 cm) skewers, skewer beef, onion and pepper alternately. Broil or grill until desired doneness is achieved.

CARAMELIZED PORK AND EGGS (Thịt heo kho với trứng)

A nutritious dish that can be served with hot steamed rice.

Ingredients (serves 4)
1 lb (450 g) pork butt with skin
1 clove garlic, crushed
¼ onion, diced
½ cup fish sauce
½ cup sugar
4 hard-boiled eggs, shelled
2 cups (16 oz/473 ml) coconut juice, fresh or canned
1 Tbsp Asian caramel syrup
2 Tbsp oil for stir-frying

① Cut pork into serving pieces. Season with garlic, onion, fish sauce and sugar. Let stand for 10 minutes.

② Heat oil in a wok, and brown pork lightly.

③ Add 1 cup coconut juice and simmer for 5 minutes.

④ Skim away scums, and add remaining coconut juice. Add boiled eggs and caramel syrup, and continue to simmer for 20 minutes until liquid is thickened.

PORK PATTY HANOI STYLE (Nem nướng Hà Nội)

Ingredients (serves 4-6)
1 lb (450 g) freshly ground pork
2 Tbsp fish sauce
1½ Tbsp chopped garlic
1 Tbsp sugar
1 Tbsp *sake*
½ Tbsp brown rice powder
1 tsp coconut juice
1 tsp white pepper
½ tsp baking powder
Banana leaves
Nuoc Cham Dipping Sauce (page 88)

Coconut juice makes this version of the hamburger distinctly Vietnamese.

① Combine ground pork and all other ingredients and stir well until smooth, preferably in food processor.

② Cut banana leaves into 2 squares of 12"×12"(30 cm), using scissors.

③ Place half of patty in center of a leaf.

④ Using a spatula, spread patty evenly.

⑤ Fold sides in to wrap up patty. Wrap again with foil. Make 2 and bake for 20 minutes in 350°F (180°C) oven.

⑥ To serve, cut into serving portions, and garnish with carrot, Asian spinach, cucumber, mint and basil leaves, if desired. Accompany with *Nuoc Cham* Dipping Sauce and wrappers.

SAIGON MEAT BALLS (Nem nướng Sài Gòn)

Brown rice powder creates a unique flavor.

Ingredients (serves 4)
1 lb (450 g) ground pork
   2 Tbsp fish sauce
   1 Tbsp sugar
   1 Tbsp chopped garlic
   2 tsp baking powder
   2 tsp brown rice powder
   1 tsp each, baking soda and white pepper
   1 tsp white pepper
Garnish:
   Mint leaves, cilantro, salad greens
Bean Dipping Sauce (page 88)

① Combine pork with all seasonings and refrigerate for 30 minutes. Shape into size of golf balls.

② In oven preheated to 350℉(180℃), bake meatballs for 20 minutes.

③ Serve skewered, if preferred, with Bean Dipping Sauce and wrappers. Garnish with herbs and salad greens.

LAMB CURRY (Cà-ri thịt trừu)

The aroma of curry stimulates the appetite.

Ingredients (serves 4)
2 lbs (900 g) boneless leg of lamb
Marinade Sauce:
   1 onion, chopped
   4 Tbsp cashew nuts, finely chopped
   8 curry leaves
   2 Tbsp plain yogurt
   2 tsp each, chopped garlic and ginger
   2 tsp each, sugar, salt, curry powder and green curry paste
   1 tsp each, black pepper and paprika
2 Tbsp olive oil for stir-frying
4 cups coconut milk
4 Thai basil leaves

① Trim fat from lamb, and cut into chunks. Combine Marinade Sauce ingredients and marinate lamb for 15-20 minutes.

② Heat olive oil in a skillet, and sauté lamb chunks for 3-4 minutes over medium high heat until browned.

③ Pour in coconut milk. Cover and simmer for 45 minutes. Adjust taste with sugar and salt. Add Thai basil leaves.

STUFFED TOFU WITH MUSHROOMS (Đậu hũ nhồi nấm)

Deep-fried *tofu* cutlets turn into a legendary Vietnamese delicacy.

Ingredients (serves 4)

20 oz (570 g) deep-fried *tofu*

Stuffing:
  4 fresh mushrooms
  2 *shiitake* mushrooms
  ¼ cup softened wood ear
    mushroom shreds
  1 green onion
  4 oz (120 g) firm *tofu* (bean curd)
  2 tsp soy sauce
  ½ tsp sesame oil
4 green onions, blanched

2 Tbsp olive oil

Cooking Sauce:
  3 Tbsp tomato ketchup
  1 tsp each, salt and pepper
  ½ tsp sugar
  ¼ tsp chopped garlic
  ½ cup coconut juice
1 tomato

Garnish:
  Green onion

① Cut deep-fried *tofu* diagonally into triangles. Make a deep slit into cut sides. Drain firm *tofu* in a colander.

② Slice *shiitake* and button mushrooms, wood ear mushrooms and chopped green onion. Chop tomato.

③ Crumble *tofu* and combine with stuffing ingredients.

④ Stuff each deep-fried *tofu* with a quartered stuffing, and tie it with green onion around each to secure.

⑤ Heat olive oil and pan-fry stuffed *tofu*, cut sides down, over medium high heat.

⑥ Add Cooking Sauce ingredients and heat until thickened. Transfer onto a serving plate, add chopped tomato and pour over remaining sauce.

BRAISED TOFU AND VEGETABLES (Đậu hũ và rau kho chay)

Pineapple adds a tropical flavor.

Ingredients (serves 4)
20 oz (570 g) cake deep-fried *tofu*, diced
½ head medium cabbage
1 carrot
4 cups button mushrooms
2 *shiitake* mushrooms
4 oz (120 g) long beans
½ cup pineapple juice
2 Tbsp pineapple chunks
5 oz (150 g) canned bamboo shoot
 tips with chili
4 oz (120 g) canned gluten *tofu*

Cooking Sauce:
 2 Tbsp sugar
 1 Tbsp chopped garlic
 ½ Tbsp soy sauce
 2 tsp salted soy beans
1 Tbsp olive oil for stir-frying

① Prepare vegetables; carrot, cabbage, and mushrooms.

② Heat olive oil and garlic in a wok. Add carrot and long beans. Stir-fry briefly and pour in pineapple juice. Cover and cook for 2 minutes.

③ Add mushrooms and cabbage, cover and cook for another 2 minutes.

④ Add deep-fried *tofu*, pineapple chunks and bamboo shoot tips, then add Cooking Sauce ingredients. Cook and stir for 2-3 minutes.

SWEET AND SOUR TOFU SPARERIBS (Đậu hũ xào kiểu sườn non)

An ideal recipe for vegetarians.

Ingredients (serves 4)
8 oz (230 g) *tofu* "ham"
4-5 linguini noodles
½ onion
Cooking Sauce:
    1 cup tomato ketchup
    2 tsp each, soy sauce and sugar
    1 tsp chopped garlic
    ½ tsp sesame oil
    2 cups coconut soda
Oil for deep-frying
Garnish
    Cilantro

① Cut onion and *tofu* "ham" into large chunks.

② Skewer each *tofu* "ham" chunk with 2 short linguini noodles.

③ Deep-fry skewered *tofu* "ham" until golden. Set aside.

④ Combine all Cooking Sauce ingredients and add fried *tofu* chunks and onion. Cook and stir over medium heat until sauce is absorbed.

SPICY TOFU CURRY (Đậu hũ xào lăng)

Tofu distinguishes this dish.

Ingredients (serves 4)

8 oz (240 g) *tofu* "ham"
2 green onions
½ red bell pepper
⅔ cup softened *saifun* noodles
¼ cup softened wood ear mushroom shreds
2 *shiitake* mushrooms
2 cloves garlic, chopped
Cooking Sauce:
  2 Tbsp sugar
  1 Tbsp each, soy sauce, whole sweet soy beans

1 Tbsp curry powder or paste
6 Tbsp water

2 Tbsp store-bought diced roasted peanuts
1 Tbsp oil for stir-frying
Garnish:
  Cilantro

① Tear *tofu* "ham" into bite-size pieces. Slice *shiitake* mushrooms, green onions and red chili pepper.

② Heat oil in a wok and add garlic. Stir-fry *tofu* "ham", red pepper and green onions. Stir in *saifun* noodles and mushrooms. Season with Cooking Sauce indredients. Sprinkle with roasted peanuts and garnish with cilantro.

Tofu "Ham"

Tofu "ham" is made by compressing *tofu* to remove most of its liquid, and marinating in soy sauce and spices. It has a smooth texture.

WOK FRIED NOODLES WITH SEAFOOD (Hủ tiếu tươi xào hải sản)

A touch of fish sauce adds zest to this dish.

Ingredients (serves 3)

½ lb (230 g) fresh flat rice noodles
6 oz (170 g) seafood, such as
   shrimp, squid, scallop
1 baby bok choy
½ carrot
1 *shiitake* mushroom
2 oz (60 g) broccoli
2 oz (60 g) bean sprouts
¼ onion
1 egg, beaten

½ Tbsp each, fish sauce and soy sauce
1 tsp sugar
¼ cup vegetable or chicken stock
1 Tbsp oil for stir-frying

① Prepare vegetables. Split bok choy into halves or quarters. Cut broccoli into flowerets. Slice carrot, onion and *shiitake* mushrooms.

② Cut fresh noodles into ½" (1.5 cm) width.

③ Heat oil and stir-fry seafood until heated through. Stir in vegetables, then beaten egg.

④ Add noodles and stir-fry. Season with fish sauce, soy sauce and sugar. Pour stock in and bring to a boil.

"THANG" NOODLES (Bún thang)

The National Dish of Vietnam.

Ingredients (serves 4)

½ lb (230 g) rice vermicelli
12 cups chicken or pork stocks (see page 89)
1 oz (30 g) dried shrimp
1 Tbsp sugar
½ Tbsp fish sauce
½ tsp fine shrimp sauce
1 egg, beaten
1 Tbsp oil
2 oz (60 g) cooked pork butt
1 Tbsp turmeric powder
3 oz (90 g) cooked chicken breast
2 oz (60 g) Vietnamese ham
4-6 fresh mint leaves

Note

There are many varieties of rice noodles, some of which are made by hand-pulled method. The cooking time depends on the thickness of the noodles. Read the description on package before cooking. If it cooks in a very short time, make sure to prepare soup and other ingredients beforehand.

① Cook rice vermicelli in boiling water for 10 - 15 minutes until softened. Drain and set aside.

② Bring chicken stock to a boil; add dried shrimp and cook for 2-3 minutes. Remove shrimp. Season the stock with sugar, fish sauce and fine shrimp sauce .

③ In a skillet or wok, heat 1T oil and pour beaten egg to make a thin omelet.

④ Cut cooked pork butt into serving pieces and coat with turmeric powder.

⑤ Cut Vietnamese ham, chicken and egg omelet into strips.

⑥ Place noodles in a large soup bowl. Top with meats, chicken, omelet and mint leaves. Just before serving, pour over hot soup stock.

TOMATO AND CRAB NOODLES (Bún riêu)

Crab meat paste adds its distinctive color to this dish.

Ingredients (serves 4)
10½ oz (300 g) rice vermicelli
12 cups chicken or pork stock
  (page 89)
¼ cup dried shrimp, soaked in water
1 tomato
1 green onion
3 oz (90 g) ground pork or chicken
  2 Tbsp store-bought crab meat paste
  ½ Tbsp fish sauce
  2 tsp sugar
  ½ tsp fine shrimp sauce
  ⅛ tsp paprika
  2 eggs, beaten

1 Tbsp fish sauce
1 Tbsp sugar

① Cook rice vermicelli in boiling water until softened. Drain and set aside. Soak dried shrimp until softened.

② Slice tomato and green onion.

③ Combine ground meat, crab meat paste, ½ Tbsp fish sauce, fine shrimp sauce, dried shrimp, sugar and paprika. Add beaten eggs, and mix in a blender. Blend well.

④ Pour meat mixture into boiling stock. Season stock with fish sauce and sugar. Add tomato. In a large soup bowl, place noodles and pour over soup.

HUE BEEF NOODLES (Bún bò Huế)

A spicy dish originated in Hue, the ancient capital of the central province.

Ingredients (serves 4)
10½ oz (300 g) rice vermicelli
Soup Base:
  12 cups beef or pork stock (page 89)
  8 oz (230 g) pork ham hock
  8 oz (230 g) beef brisket
  4 oz (120 g) pineapple slices
  ½ cup fish sauce
  2 Tbsp sugar
  1 stalk lemon grass
  ½ tsp fine shrimp sauce

Spicy Chili Sauce:
  2 Tbsp oil
  1 Tbsp fish sauce
  1 Tbsp lemon grass,chopped
  1 tsp paprika
  1 tsp garlic,chopped
  1 tsp chili paste
  ½ tsp chili powder
Garnish:
  Cilantro

① Prepare soup stock. In a pot, heat Soup Base ingredients to a boil. Reduce heat and cook for 15 minutes, skimming fat that floats.

② Combine Spicy Chili Sauce ingredients.

③ Add Spicy Chili Sauce to pot. Simmer for another 15 minutes. Remove meats and slice. Strain stock.

④ While cooking soup, cook rice vermicelli in boiling water, and drain. Place it in a soup dish. Place meats as topping. Pour over soup and garnish with cilantro.

67

SAIGON NOODLES (Bún suông)

Noodle dishes are never the same after trying this delicacy from Saigon.

Ingredients (serves 4)
8 oz (230 g) rice vermicelli
12 cups chicken or pork stock (page 89)
1 lb (450 g) ham hock
4 oz (120 g) cooked crab meat
8 medium shrimp
8 slices cooked shrimp paste (page 18)
Seasoning:
　½ cup fish sauce
　1 Tbsp sugar
　1 Tbsp crab paste with bean oil (in a jar), optional for red color
　1 tsp paprika
Dash white pepper

1 egg white

Garnish:
　Cilantro

① Cook ham hock in chicken or pork stock for 1 hour over medium heat, occasionally skimming foam. Add Seasoning, then stir in beaten egg white.

② Shell and cook shrimp in boiling water. Slice pork, shrimp and cooked shrimp paste into serving pieces.

③ Cook rice vermicelli in boiling water. Place cooked noodles in a serving bowl. Top with pork, shrimp and cooked shrimp paste. Pour soup over noodles and garnish with cilantro.

HANOI NOODLES (Bún chả Hà Nội)

People of Hanoi are fond of meats, hence the name.

Ingredients (serves 4)
½ lb (230 g) rice vermicelli
1 lb (450 g) pork tenderloin
Marinade Sauce:
 5 Tbsp fish sauce
 2 Tbsp each, honey and chopped green onion
 3 tsp sugar
 2 tsp chopped garlic
 Dash black pepper
1 Tbsp store-bought diced roasted peanuts
Garnish:
 Asian spinach
 10 mint leaves
Nuoc Cham Dipping Sauce (page 88)

① Combine Marinade Sauce ingredients. Slice pork thinly and marinate for 15 minutes. Cook rice vermicelli, immerse in water and drain.

② Skewer pork slices by squeezing and pressing each. Make 8 skewers.

③ Hold skewers between a gridiron, and grill until done. Set aside to cool.

④ On a serving platter, mound noodles and top with grilled meat. Sprinkle with roasted peanuts. Arrange Asian spinach and mint leaves. Serve with *Nuoc Cham* Dipping Sauce.

69

BEEF PHO (Phở bò)

The most well-known Vietnamese noodle soup.

Ingredients (serves 4)

10 oz (300 g) rice noodles (*pho*)
12 cups beef stock (page 89)
 4 oz (120 g) lean beef
 2 cinnamon sticks
 2 oz (60 g) fresh ginger
 4 whole anise stars
10 whole cloves
 4 shallots, broiled until browned
¼ cup fish sauce
 2 Tbsp sugar
½ Tbsp salt
 1 *pho* soup cube ,optional

Garnish:
 Onion slices
 Cilantro

Rice Noodles (*Pho*)

① In boiling stock, cook lean beef together with all other ingredients over low heat, skimming occasionally. When beef is cooked, remove and slice thinly.

② Cook rice noodles (*pho*) in boiling water, drain and transfer into a serving bowl. Top with beef slices, and garnish with onion and cilantro. Pour over soup.

Pho is possibly one of Vietnam's most famous rice noodle and its dishes. *Pho* is slightly thicker and flatter than the common rice noodles and is cut into pieces. If unavailable, substitute with regular rice vermicelli or egg noodles.

CHICKEN PHO (Phở gà)

The chicken version of the delicately seasoned broth and noodles.

Ingredients (serves 4)

10½ oz (300 g) rice noodles (*pho*)
12 cups chicken stock (page 89)
　1 whole chicken or
　　1 lb (450 g) chicken breast
　10 whole cloves
　5 whole anises star
　2 cinnamon sticks
　¼ cup fish sauce
　2 Tbsp sugar
　½ Tbsp salt
　1 stalk celery

　1 *pho* soup cube, optional
　1 store-bought salted lemon
　4 shallots, broiled until browned
Garnish:
　4 slices fresh ginger, shredded
　Cilantro

① In a large pot, cook chicken in chicken stock with rest of ingredients until done for about 30 minutes over medium heat, skimming foam. Remove chicken. Strain stock.

② Cook rice noodles (*pho*). Slice chicken thinly. Place noodles in a serving bowl, top with chicken, shredded fresh ginger root and chopped cilantro. Pour hot stock over.

Pho Soup Cube

A popular bouillon cube used also as a seasoning in Vietnam. One *pho* soup cube makes about 3 cups of stock.

SEAFOOD NOODLES (Mì nước & hải sản)

Delicious noodles, artfully garnished with an assortment of seafood.

Ingredients (serves 4)

14 oz (400 g) egg noodles
12 cups chicken or pork stock
  (page 89)
  ¼ cup fish sauce
  1 Tbsp dry shrimp
  1 Tbsp sugar
  1 tsp salt
  1 dried medium squid
8 shrimp, shelled and deveined
3 oz (90 g) calamari, cut into strips
3 oz (90 g) crab meat or claws

Garnish:
  Cilantro
  Green onion, chopped
  Garlic chives
Lime wedges

① Cook dried squid in stock for 10 minutes, skimming occasionally. Then cook shrimp, calamari and crab meat in same stock just until done.

② Cook noodles in boiling water, drain and transfer into a serving bowl.

③ Arrange seafood over noodles and garnish with chopped green onion, cilanrto and garlic chives. Pour hot soup over them. Serve accompanied with lime wedges.

YOUNG COCONUT RICE (Cơm trắng nấu với dừa tưởi)

Rice is the staple grain of the whole Asia.

Ingredients (serves 4)
3 cups jasmine, brown or Japanese short grain rice
4 cups water
2 cups coconut juice
Pinch salt
1 cinnamon stick
4 whole cloves

Coconut Juice

① Rinse rice and drain. In a rice cooker, mix rice, water, and coconut juice.

② Turn on rice cooker, and when half-way through cooking, after about 15 minutes, add salt, whole cloves and cinnamon stick. Cover and continue to cook.

Coconut juice is the clear liquid in the center of young coconut.

ROYAL RICE (Cơm hòang gia)

A lovely way to serve seasoned rice.

Ingredients (serves 4)

1½ cups jasmine rice, rinsed and drained
  2 cups coconut juice
½ cup diced Chinese barbecue pork
½ cup diced Vietnamese ham
1 salted egg (use only chopped yolk)
⅓ cup chopped onion
½ cup green peas, cooked
Thin omelet (makes 4):
  2 egg, beaten
  2 tsp cornstarch
  4 tsp oil

1 tsp crushed garlic
½ Tbsp soy sauce
2 Tbsp oil for stir-frying
Garnish:
  4 Pears

Preparation

Cook rice with coconut juice in a rice cooker.

① Prepare salted egg yolk, barbecued pork, Vietnamese ham and onion accordingly.

② Heat 1 tsp oil in a non-stick skillet, and pour in ¼ of egg mixed with cornstarch, and make a thin egg omelet. Remove and set aside. Make 4 thin omelets.

③ Heat oil in a wok, and saute garlic and onion. Add cooked rice, ham, egg yolk and green peas. Cook and stir well, then season with soy sauce.

④ Spread omelet, and place one-fourth of seasoned rice. Fold up all sides, and place upside down in a serving dish. Make a crisscross cut and open "parcel". Garnish with pear.

EMPRESS RICE (Cơm hòang hậu)

A popular favorite, this dish is perfect for special occasions.

Ingredients (serves 2)

1 cup jasmine rice, rinsed and drained
  2 4"(10 cm) Asian vanilla leaves
  2 cups coconut juice
½ cup each, diced Asian sausage
¼ cup diced Asian ham
½ cup diced cooked ckicken
2 oz (60 g) sliced long beans
½ cup dried shrimp, soaked in water
2 salted egg (use only chopped yolks)
2 thin omelets (page 74)
1 tsp chopped garlic

5 quail eggs, hard-boiled
½ tsp each, sugar, salt, pepper, soy sauce
2 Tbsp oil for stir-frying

Preparation
Cook rice with vanilla leaves and coconut juice in a rice cooker.

① In a non-stick skillet, make 2 thin omelets, and shred finely. Cut up all remaining ingredients except for quail eggs.

② Heat oil in a wok, and stir-fry all ingredients except quail eggs. Season with sugar, salt, pepper and soy sauce.

③ Place hard-boiled quail eggs in a rice bowl or mold.

④ Pless down the meat mixture to line the bowl. Add cooked rice and press hard. Turn over to unmold.

EIGHT-JEWEL RICE (Cơm bát bửu)

The presentation makes this dish a real conversation piece.

Ingredients (serves 2)

1 cup jasmine rice, rinsed and drained
  2 4"(10 cm) Asian vanilla leaves
  2 cups water
½ cup sliced Asian barbecued pork
2 *shiitake* mushrooms, sliced
½ cup Vietnamese ham strips
6 prawns, deveined
2 oz (60 g) crab meat
¼ cup sliced onion
1 salted egg (use only yolk)
1 thin omelet (page 74)
½ Tbsp soy sauce
Salt and pepper
1 Tbsp oil for stir-frying
4-6 fresh lotus leaves
Garnish:
  Carrot flowers

① Cut ingredients into julienne strips.

② Heat oil in a skillet or wok and stir-fry prawns, crab meat, cut ingredients and rice. Season with salt, pepper and soy sauce.

Preparation
Cook rice with vanilla leaves and water in a rice cooker.

③ Blanch lotus leaves in boiling water, then plunge into cold water; wipe dry.

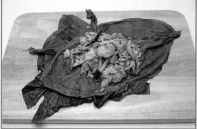

④ Spread lotus leaves, and mound a half portion of fried rice in center.

⑤ Fold up all sides to resemble a parcel and steam for 10-15 minutes. Make 2. Serve garnished with carrot flowers, if you prefer.

CLAY POT RICE (Cơm tay cầm)

Twice cooked rice gives a light, fluffy texture.

Ingredients (serves 4)
1 cup jasmine rice
  2 cups chicken stock (page 89)
5 oz (140 g) chicken livers, cooked
5 oz (140 g) chicken, cooked
1 carrot, diced
½ onion, chopped
2-3 *shiitake* mushrooms, sliced
¼ cup softened wood ear
  mushroom shreds
½ Tbsp shredded ginger

Cooking Sauce:
  1 cup chicken stock
  1 Tbsp soy sauce
  1 tsp sugar
  ¼ tsp sesame oil
2 Tbsp oil for stir-frying

Preparation
Cook rice with chicken stock in a rice cooker.

① Prepare ingredients by slicing chicken livers and chicken, and cutting vegetables. In a pot, cook rinsed rice with chicken stock.

② Heat oil in a skillet, and stir-fry all vegetables, chicken livers and chicken. Add Cooking Sauce ingredients. After rice is cooked, mix with all cooked ingredieuts.

③ Transfer into a clay pot. Bake in an oven preheated to 375°F (190 ℃) for 10-15 minutes. Serves hot.

HALF-MOON PAN FRIED CREPE (Bánh xeo)

Ingredients (makes 4)
Batter:
  2 cups *Bot Do Banh Xeo* flour mix
  1 cup water
  ¼ cup beer
  1 Tbsp coconut milk
  1 tsp turmeric powder
  ⅛ tsp salt
  ¼ tsp baking powder
24 small shrimp
¼ lb (230 g) pork, sliced
3 oz (90 g) bean sprouts
1 carrot, cut into strips
¼ small onion, sliced
Green onion, optional
2 Tbsp oil
Nuoc Cham Dipping Sauce (page 88)

A variety of fillings, wrapped in a crepe.

① Combine all Batter ingredients in a bowl. Rest it for 1 hour.

② Slice pork, carrot and onion. Clean and shell shrimp.

③ Heat 1 Tbsp oil in a skillet, and cook meat, shrimp, carrot and onion; set aside.

④ Grease skillet lightly, and pour a quarter portion of batter into it. Make a thin omelet-like a crepe. Place a portion of cooked ingredients over crepe. Sprinkle with bean sprouts and chopped green onion.

⑤ Fold in half. Make 4. Transfer onto a serving plate, and serve with *Nuoc Cham* Dipping Sauce.

Bot Do Banh Xeo Flour Mix

A pre-mixed flour for making pancakes, sold in Asian food markets. It can be substituted with rice flour and cornstarch in the ratio of 6:1.

VIETNAMESE CRAB QUICHE (Chả cua)

An elegant and colorful hot dish, which can be served at any banquet table.

Ingredients (serves 4)
4 eggs, lightly beaten
3 oz (90 g) ground pork
2 oz (60 g) crab meat
1 Tbsp sliced green onion
½ cup softened *saifun* noodles, cut into 1"(2.5 cm) pieces
¼ cup softened wood ear mushrooms
Salt and pepper
½ tsp sugar
1 Tbsp fish sauce
2 egg yolks for glaze

Saifun Noodles
(bean threads/cellophene noodles)

① Preheat an oven to 325°F(160°C). In a bowl, combine all ingredients except for egg yolks well.

② Pour into a 8½"(22 cm), greased pie plate, and bake for 20-25 minutes until center is almost set. Brush egg yolks over surface, and bake for another 5 minutes.

These white noodles are made from mung beans and potato starch. Dried noodles increase in volume as they cooks, three or four times, depending on the kind.

VIETNAMESE SANDWICH (Bánh mì thịt Việt Nam)

Various fillings give this sandwich a Vietnamese flavor.

Ingredients
Baguette or French bread, and fillings including:
Vietnamese ham
Pork ham
Daikon radish
Green onion
Cucumber
Cilantro
Vietnamese paté
Mayonnaise
Vietnamese soy sauce
Salt and pepper

① Cut baguette or French bread into 6"(15 cm) lengths, then make a deep slit into each piece. Slice Vietnamese ham, pate and pork ham. Cut carrot and *daikon* into julienne strips, and sprinkle with salt and pepper; let stand for 5 minutes until supple. Toss them with soy sauce, and squeeze out excess moisture.

② Open the bread and spread mayonnaise inside, and sandwich layers of meats and marinated vegetables. Garnish with green onion.

BANANA AND BREAD PUDDING (Bánh chuối)

A great dessert, warm or cold.

Ingredients (for 8½"/22 cm baking pan or dish)
4 ripe bananas
10 slices white sandwich bread
1½ cups coconut milk
½ cup sugar
½ cup coconut flakes
⅓ cup condensed milk
1 egg

① Preheat oven to 350 ℉(180℃) .Cut bananas into ¼"(5-6 mm) thin slices. Cut up bread and toss well with coconut milk, sugar, coconut flakes, condensed milk, and egg.

② In a 8½"(22 cm) baking dish, spread half amount of mixture, and place banana slices evenly over it.

③ Add remaining mixture, and arrange remaining banana slices on top. Bake in oven for 45-50 minutes. Let cool before cutting.

JELLO IN FRUIT CUPS (Trái cây và thạch)

The combination of coconut and green vanilla leaves excites the taste buds.

Ingredients (serves 4-6)
⅓ oz (10 g) agar-agar strips
    or
¼ oz (6 g) agar-agar powder
  3 cups water
  ⅔ cup sugar

2-3 oz (60-90 g) green vanilla leaves
1 oz (30 ml) coconut milk
1 oz (30 ml) espresso

Fruit Cup:
Pineapple, papaya, mango, etc.

Preparation
Soften agar-agar strips, by covering with water for 30 minutes at least. Make "fruit cups" by scooping out seeds and some flesh of fruit of your choice.

① Grind vanilla leaves.

② Wrap in a cheesecloth and squeeze out juice to yield 2 Tbsp (30ml) juice.

③ Drain soaked agar-agar, squeeze out water and measure to fill ½ cup. If using powder, skip this step.

④ Put the measured water in a saucepan, add agar-agar (sprinkle, if using powder type), and bring to a slow boil. Continue to cook 1-2 minutes until clear, stir in sugar, and remove from heat.

⑤ Place espresso, coconut milk, vanilla juice in individual bowls. Stir in ⅓ aga-agar mixture into each. Pour mixture into fruit "cups," and chill for 1 hour or until set.

Agar-agar

A seaweed extract used widely as a setting agent in Asia, just as gelatin powder in the West. Aga-agar comes in various forms including strips, sticks and powder. If unavailable, it can be substituted with 1 package of gelatin powder, but the method and result are quite different. Agar-agar has to be parboiled, and once set, it never becomes runny.

JACKFRUIT AND COCONUT ICE CREAM (Kem lạnh dừa và mít)

Roasted coconut flakes make this ice cream refreshing and tasty.

Ingredients (makes 2 qts/2 L)
1 cup canned coconut milk
½ cup cow's milk
2 cups sugar
Pinch salt
2 cups heavy cream
½ cup half and half
½ tsp vanilla extract
¼ cup canned or frozen jackfruit
¼ cup roasted coconut

① In a small saucepan, place cow's milk and ½ cup of upper, creamy portion of coconut milk and warm over medium heat. Do not boil.

② Remove from heat, and stir in sugar and a pinch of salt. Add remaining coconut milk, heavy cream, half and half and vanilla extract.

③ Pour milk mixture into an ice cream maker. Put in a good amount of ice cubes around the inner pot, and turn on. Let run for about 1 hour.

④ Cut up jackfruit, and add to ice cream together with roasted coconut. Keep in freezer overnight or until serving.

LYCHEE AND LOTUS SEED DESSERT (Chè hạt sen và trái vải)

A traditional Vietnamese dessert, combining two different textures and flavors.

Ingredients (serves 2-3)
8 oz (230 g) canned lychees
Lotus seeds in a 1:1 ratio
  with lychees (camed or dried)
1 Tbsp sugar

6 cups water
2 cups sugar
2 vanilla leaves

Lotus Seeds

The fresh lotus seeds become white and soft when boiled in water. Average size is about ½"(1.5 cm) in diameter.

① Coat lotus seeds with 1 Tbsp of sugar.

② Fill each lychee hole with a sugar-coated lotus seed.

③ In a pot, bring water, sugar and vanilla leaves to a boil.

④ Add stuffed lychees and cook over medium heat for about 20 minutes. Serve warm.

FLYING DRAGON SHAKE (Sinh tố trái thăng long)

Sumptuous dragon fruit imparts a memorable texture and flavor.

Ingredients (serves 4)
2 packages frozen dragon fruit
1 oz (30 ml) orange liqueur
1 oz (30 ml) grenadine syrup
1 cup ice cubes

Dragon Fruit

① Split dragon fruit in half, peel and cut flesh into chunks.

② In a blender, put dragon fruit, grenadine syrup, orange liqueur, and ice cubes. Blend for 45 seconds and serve immediately.

Dragon fruit comes in two colors: pink and yellow. The flesh is sweet. Best to use frozen. Do not defrost.

GINGER LEMONADE (Nước chanh & gừng)

A unique and refreshing cold drink, and a favorite at Andre's restaurant.

Ingredients (makes 2 cups)
1 oz (30 g) fresh ginger root
1 cup sugar
1 cup water

2 lemons
2 limes
Lime wedges

① Peel and slice ginger root into ¼"(5-6 mm) thicknesses. Chop slices in a mortar or crush in a garlic press.

② In a small saucepan, put sugar and water, and bring to a boil. Add chopped or crushed ginger.

③ Cook for 30 minutes until the liquid becomes syrupy. Remove from heat and let stand to cool.

④ Squeeze lemons and limes. Blend with ginger syrup, and serve with ice cubes and lime wedges.

DIPPING SAUCES

There is a variety of dipping sauces. Choose which-ever you prefer to use in main and side dishes.

NUOC CHAM DIPPING SAUCE

Makes about 1½ cups
1 cup boiling water
⅓ cup fish sauce
⅓ cup sugar
2 Tbsp lime juice
 (1 lime, squeezed)
½ Tbsp peeled leek in vinegar
1 tsp chili paste
1 carrot, shredded

Combine all ingredients. This sauce keeps up to three weeks, if refrigerated.

NOUC CHAM VINAIGRETTE

Makes about 1¼ cups
1 cup *NUOC CHAM* DIPPING SAUCE (see above)
¼ cup Japanese rice vinegar
1 Tbsp lime juice
 (½ lime, squeezed)
1 Tbsp vegetable oil
2 cloves garlic, sliced

Combine all ingredients well.

SHRIMP PASTE DIPPING SAUCE

Makes about 1 cup
¼ cup canned coconut soda
4 Tbsp lime juice
(2 limes, squeezed)
3 Tbsp sugar
3 heap Tbsp shrimp paste
2 tsp chili paste
1 tsp chopped garlic
1 Tbsp roasted shallot, optional

Combine all ingredients. Good for fish seviche and lotus root salad.

BEAN DIPPING SAUCE

Makes about 2¼ cups
1½ cups water
1 cup chopped onion
½ cup hoisin sauce
¼ cup bean sauce
¼ cup plum sauce
¼ cup sugar
2 Tbsp creamy peanut butter

Combine all ingredients except peanut butter in a small saucepan. Cook over medium heat until onion becomes soft. Stir in peanut butter. Let stand to cool.

TAMARIND DIPPING SAUCE

Makes about 1 cup
2½ oz (70 g) preserved tamarind
½ cup coconut soda
3 Tbsp sugar
1 Tbsp garlic, chopped or minced

Stir all ingredients in a saucepan until smooth, and cook until thoroughly blended. Strain to make a smooth sauce. Good for seafood, chicken and vegetable dishes.

PINEAPPLE DIPPING SAUCE

Makes about 1½ cups
1½ cups crushed pineapple
¼ cups coconut soda
2 Tbsp lime juice
(1 lime, squeezed)
2 tsp chopped garlic
2 tsp anchovy paste
1 tsp chili paste

Stir all ingredients in a bowl. Store in refrigerator until serving time. Good for grilled or steamed fish and broiled shrimp.

SOUP STOCKS

The way to make delicious soup stock is dependent on the amount of attention to details such as controlling the heat and skimming froth, scum or fat during the simmering stage. This requires a certain amount of patience.

However, instant or ready-made soup stocks are available. So, it may be convenient to have some of them. As a general guide, 1 can (46 oz/1300 g) of chicken or beef broth makes about 6 cups of broth. 1 cube bouillon of chicken, beef or vegetable, makes 1 cup of broth.

BASIC BEEF OR PORK SOUP STOCK

Makes about 12 cups
4½ lbs (2 kg) beef bones or pork spareribs
12½ cups water

1 Trim off excess fat from beef bones or pork ribs.
2 In a large saucepan, put bones or ribs with water, and bring to a boil. Reduce heat to medium low, and simmer for 45 minutes to 1 hour. Skim off the froth, scum or fat while simmering.
3 Discard bones or ribs. Let it cool, then keep in the refrigerator for several hours or overnight. Remove hardened fat off from the surface.

CHICKEN SOUP STOCK

Makes about 12 cups
4½ lbs (2 kg) chicken backbone, neck and wings
      or
1 whole chicken, cut up
½" (1.5 cm) cube fresh ginger
1 green onion, sliced into 1" (2.5 cm) length
12½ cups water

1 In a large saucepan, put all ingredients and bring to a boil. Skim off scum and fat. Reduce heat to low and simmer for 1 - 1½ hours. Skim occasionally while simmering, uncovered.
2 Strain stock through a sieve.
3 When cooled, keep in the refrigerator for several hours or overnight. Remove hardened fat off from the surface.
(Use the stock as recipe calls for, or pour stock into ice cube tray for later uses.)

SEASONED SOUP STOCK

Makes about 12 cups
12 cups beef or pork stock
½ cup fish sauce
2 Tbsp sugar
2" (5 cm) length lemon grass

1 In a saucepan, add all ingredients and bring to a boil.
2 Remove lemon grass.

SHRIMP FLAVORED SOUP STOCK

Makes about 12 cups
¼ cup dried shrimp
1 Tbsp chopped green onion
2 Tbsp crab meat paste (in a jar)
½ Tbsp fish sauce
2 tsp sugar
½ tsp fine shrimp paste or sauce
⅛ tsp paprika
12½ cups water

1 In a large saucepan, put dried shrimp, chopped onion, and water. Bring to a boil, then reduce heat to low, and simmer for 15 minutes. Strain stock and discard shrimp and green onion.
2 Reheat stock and add remaining ingredients.
Variation
Any leftover vegetable scraps or peels can be added to dried shrimp and green onion.

FISH SOUP STOCK

Makes about 12 cups
1-2 fish heads
Some fish bones
1-2 dried chili
1 stalk celery
½ onion
1 slice fresh ginger
1 Tbsp sugar
1 tsp salt
13-14 cups water

1 In a large saucepan, put all ingredients with water, and bring to a boil. Skim froth that floats.
2 Reduce heat to low and simmer for 45 minutes. Strain through a sieve.

G L O S S A R Y

#1

basil

ASIAN SPINACH (*Rau muong*)
This leafy green vegetable has a crunchy hollow stem, which the Vietnamese use in salads and soups. Can be substituted with spinach or water cress, if not available.

BANANA LEAVES
The large leaves of the banana tree are used for lining plates or wrapping various foods for cooking to improve flavor. They are usually sold fresh or frozen in Asian grocery stores. Wipe the leaves with a damp cloth before using.

#2

coconut milk

BASIL (*Rau que*) #1
Asian basil and sweet basils have a faint anise seed flavor. Holy basil has more pungent flavor. Hairy basil has a lemon scent and is slightly peppery. The basil you find in Asian market is Thai basil with shiny green leaves and stems sometimes purple. European basil has a different from than Asian variety. Basil is best to be used fresh.

BEAN PASTE
Soybean sauce made from soy beans, chili pepper, and sometimes garlic.

#3

crab paste

CURRY LEAVES
The hardwood tree with the shiny green leaves grow in South Asian countries. The full curry flavor is released when the leaves are bruised. The leaves impart a destinctive flavor.

#4

dragon fruit

CHILI PLUM SAUCE (*Nuoc trai dao*)
A sauce made from plums and apricots as well as vinegar, sugar and chili pepper.

#5

fine shrimp sauce

CHILI SAUCE FOR CHICKEN (*Tuong ot chua ngot*)
This thick red sauce is made from red chili, sugar, garlic and salt.

CHINESE SAUSAGE (*Lap xuong*)
This sweet, cured pork sausage is about 6 " (15 cm) in length. It can be refrigerated up to one month, or frozen up to several months.

CILANTRO (*Ngo*)
Also known as coriander, this leafy green parsley plant is used for both cooking and as a garnish.

COCONUT MILK (*Nuoc cot dua*) #2
Coconut milk is made by grating the meat of a mature, fresh coconut, combining it with hot water, and squeezing through a filter to extract the liquid. Coconut milk can be purchased in cans.

COCONUT SODA
The clear liquid in the center of young coconut is referred to as coconut water or soda.

CRAB PASTE (*Gach cua*) #3
The cooked crab meat is grilled to make paste and mixted with several different spices to release a delicate flavor.

CURRY PASTE (*Ca ri dau*)
This paste is made by blending chili pepper, lemon grass, garlic, salt, galanga, shallots, Kaffir lime leaves, coriander seeds, pepper and cumin.

CURRY POWDER
A blend of many different spices, often used to make curry marinades.

DRAGON FRUIT (*Thanh long*) #4
Dragon fruit comes in pink or yellow. The flesh is sweet and refreshing, and is best eaten chilled.

DRIED SHRIMP (*Tom kho*)
It is widely used in cooking. These dried tiny shrimp should be soaked in warm water to soften before use.

FINE SHRIMP SAUCE (*Mam tom*) #5
A very thick paste made from salted shrimp. It has a very strong pungent flavor but becomes more mellow when cooked. It will keep indefinitely in a tightly sealed jar. Sour Shrimp Paste. (*Gia Vi Nau Canh Chua*) is also available.

FISH SAUCE (*Nuoc mam*)
Known as Nuoc Mam in Vietnam, this sauce is made from salted fish. There are many varieties of fish sauce, including those made from shrimp, anchovy, and squid. It will keep indefinitely on the shelf.

FIVE SPICE POWDER (*Ngu vi huong*)
A Chinese spice combination of fennel seeds, cinnamon, cloves, ginger and star anise.

GARLIC (*Toi*)
An indispensable ingredient in Veitnam cooking, it is available in several varieties, some with very white papery skin, some with pink and white skin and some creamy in color.

HOISIN SAUCE (*Tuong ngot*)
This pungent, sweet condiment is made from soy beans, spices, chili and sugar. It can be kept refrigerated for about 6 months.

JACKFRUIT (*Nit*)
A large, green fruit with a tough, nubby skin, which reveals a yellow, segmented flesh when opened. It has a taste that is naturally sweet .

JAPANESE RICE VINEGAR
This distilled white vinegar has a delicate flavor and sweetness.

JICAMA (*Cu san, Munh kaew*) #6
Jicama is used in stir-fries, salads, fillins and soups. It has a crunchy texture, and resembles a large turnip.

LEMON GRASS (*Xa*) #7
A tall, strong and graceful grass found in warm climates. The plant has a tough fibrous stem which releases a very delicate, refreshing aroma resembling that of a lemon.

LIME #8
Fresh lime is used widely in Vietnamese dishes.

LYCHEE (*Vai*)
Fresh lychee is a fruit with scaly red skin about 1"(2.5 cm) in diameter, the size of small plum. Once shelled, the flesh is pearly white and has a perfume scent. It comes both canned and fresh.

#6

jicama

MAGGI SEASONING (*Nuoc tuong maggi*)
Maggi seasoning consists of water, salt, gluten, sugar and some spices.

NOODLES #7
Noodles used in Vietnam cooking can be made of wheat, rice flour and/or mung beans. They are available both fresh and dried in various shapes and sizes.

lemon grass

Rice Noodles (*pho*) #9
Rice noodles are made from whole grains of rice. They come in various widths from the very thin thread-like type known as rice vermicelli to the rice sticks which are 3/8" (1 cm) wide. Dried rice noodles can be stored in the cooler cabinets almost indefinitely. In Vietnam, rice noodle soup is the standard breakfast.

#8

lime

To prepare rice noodles, put dried rice noodles in a large bowl filled with hot water and leave for 5-10 minutes or until softened, stirring once or twice to separate the strands from sticking together as they soften.

Plain Wheat Noodles/Egg Noodles #10
Wheat noodles are made from wheat flour and water. They come in flat or round shapes with various thickness.
Egg noodles are made from wheat flour, water and egg.

#9

rice noodles

To cook either plain wheat or egg noodles, cook noodles in boiling water. Cooking time depends on the thickness of noodles and quantity and also whether the noodles will be cooked in a soup or served as a side dish. Generally it takes about 3 minutes of cooking time, and in the process, it might be necessary to drain out starchy water and to add more water towards the end. Fresh noodles may need less cooking time, about 1 minute.

#10

egg noodles

#11

saifun noodles

#12

oyster sauce

#13

papaya

#14

plum sauce

Saifun **Noodles** (*Mien*)
Bean threads/cellophane noodles
These transparent, thread-like noodles are made from mung bean flour, and are firm, brittle and resilient. To separate the strands into small portions, place in a plastic or paper bag to avoid splattering on the floor.

To prepare *saifun* noodles, soak them in hot water for 10-15 minutes until softened. For faster results, place cellophane noodles in a large pot filled with water and bring to a boil. Turn off heat and remove from stove. Leave for 2-3 minutes or until softened. Then using scissors, cut the noodles into short length for easy handling. Since the noodles have no taste by themselves, cook with other foods and add rather strong seasonings to give off a wonderful flavor and texture. They retain their original shape without becoming soggy.

Dried noodles increase in volume as it cooks, three to four times, depending on the kind.

OYSTER SAUCE (*Dau hau*) #12
A savory sauce made from oyster extract. Usually sold in bottles, it will keep for several months when refrigerated.

PAPAYA (*Du du*) #13
The ripe, green papaya is often peeled and shredded for use in green papaya salad.

PLUM SAUCE (*Nuoc trai dao*) #14
A sauce made from plums and apricots combined with vinegar, sugar and chili pepper.

RICE
Rice has been cultivated for a thousand years in Southern Asia as the staple grain that are eaten on daily basis. Rice requires a wet and warm climate for its cultivation. However, agricultural advancements have made it such that rice could be produced in other climatic conditions.

The type, texture and flavor of rice depend on the climate. There are many varieties of rice that are available today. The varieties of rice can be broadly classified as follows:

White Rice
Short or long white rice, with its husk, bran and germ removed, are light and fluffy when cooked. Among the two, short grain rice retains moisture better. Among the varieties of white rice, Basmati (long grain rice), and Jasmine rice (fragrant rice) are especially well known. Both have a mild flavor, especially jasmine rice which has a delicate jasmine scent.

Brown Rice
Brown, short and long grain rice with its outer husk removed. It gives a chewy yet nutty flavor when cooked because of the presence of bran and germ. Those are excellent sources of dietary fibers, vitamins and minerals.

Black Rice
Black, short and long grain rice are cultivated mainly in Thailand and are widely used in Thai cooking including desserts.

Glutinous Rice
Black, white, pinkish-red or sometimes purplish-black rice is also known as sweet or sticky rice. White glutinous rice is stickier than regular white short grain rice. Black glutinous rice has a nutty flavor.

It is difficult to give a definite cooking method for cooking plain rice because each type requires individual process.

However, as a general rule, add water to rice grains using a ratio of two to one. Rice increases in volume as it cooks, twice to three times or more, depending on the kind of rice used. Cooked rice becomes either firm and fluffy, or soft and sticky.

Raw rice should be kept in an airtight container in a dry, cool place away from direct sunlight. To retain the aroma of rice, use within 3-4 months from purchase.

G L O S S A R Y

RICE FLOUR (*Bot gao*)

The rice is finely milled to make into powder. The texture is similar to that of corn flour. The rice flour is used to thicken sauces, to make rice paper and the dough for dumplings.

RICE PAPER (*Banh trang*) #15

Made from a batter of rice flour, water and salt. It is a round sheet, and dried in the sun on bamboo racks, which leaves a cross-hatched imprint. Used to wrap a wide variety of rolls, the paper must be soaked in water or can be placed on damp dish towels and brushed with water.

SALTED SOYBEANS (*Tuong hot mang*)

Soft soybeans made from soybeans, water, sugar, salt and ginger.

SESAME OIL #16

It is made from sesame seed which are rich in oil and protein. This oil has slightly nutty flavor that enhances sauces, salads and seafood.

SHIITAKE MUSHROOMS

Both fresh and dried *shiitake* mushrooms can be obtained. Dried one should be soaked in water before using. Fresh mushrooms have a distinctive, appealing "woody-fruity" flavor. The best ones have a thick, brown velvet cap and firm flesh.

SNOW PEAS

These flat, edible pea pods are sometimes called Chinese pea pods. They have a delicate taste and come fresh or frozen.

SOY SAUCE (*Nuoc tuong*) #17

Soy sauce is made from soybeans and salt. It is the primary seasoning in Asian cooking. It is used for simmered foods, dressing, soups and many kinds of cooking. Ordinary soy sauce is dark, but one which has a light color is also available.

SUGAR CANE

Sugar cane is available canned and sometimes fresh, and its outer skin should be peeled before use.

TAMARIND (*Me*) #18

The long, bean-shaped, tart-flavored, brown fruit of the tamarind tree, which, when it is dried, is often used to impart sourness to a dish.

TAMARIND POWDER (*Bot me nau canh chua*)

This seasoning is made by blending citrus acid, sugar, tamarind, sugar, onion and tomato powder.

TARO ROOT (*Khoai mon / Khoaiso*)

A barrel-shaped oval root, with hairy, brown skin and white flesh purple/brown fibers. Resembles water chestnuts when it is cooked.

TOFU

The solid curd of soybean milk. Fresh bean curd is sold packed in water. Several varieties of *tofu*, including *tofu* sheets and deep-fried *tofu* are available in Asian markets.

TOFU "HAM"

This smooth textured, *tofu*'s ham is made of fresh *tofu*, which is compressed to remove moisture, then marinated in soy sauce and five-spice powder.

TOFU SHEETS OR ROLLS

Formed from the *tofu*-making process, these sheets should be soaked in hot water until soft, rinsed and cut into the desired size before using.

TURMERIC

When fresh, the turmeric root resembles ginger root in appearance, but not in flavor. Turmeric is more readily available in powder form in most Asian grocery stores.

WOOD EAR MUSHROOMS

Also called "cloud ear mushroom", this irregularly shaped fungus has a delicate taste. It comes dried and should be soaked in warm water to soften. Can be kept indefinitely on shelf.

rice paper

sesame oil

soy sauce

tamarind

CONVERSION TABLES

1 cup is equivalent to 240 ml in our recipes:

1 American cup = 240 ml = 8 American fl oz
1 Australian cup = 250 ml = 8 Australian fl oz
1 British cup = 200 ml = 7 British fl oz
1 Japanese cup = 200 ml

1 tablespoon = 15 ml
1 teaspoon = 5 ml

Liquid Measures

milliliters $\times$ 0.034 = ounces
ounces $\times$ 29.57 = milliliters

cups	spoons	ounces	milliliters
$\frac{1}{48}$ cup	1 tsp	$\frac{1}{16}$ oz	5 ml
$\frac{1}{16}$ cup	1 Tbsp	$\frac{1}{2}$ oz	15 ml
$\frac{1}{4}$ cup	4 Tbsp	2 oz	59 ml
$\frac{1}{2}$ cup	8 Tbsp	4 oz	118 ml
1 cup	16 Tbsp	8 oz	236 ml
1$\frac{1}{4}$ cups		10 oz	296 ml(300 ml)
1$\frac{3}{4}$ cups		14 oz	414 ml
2 cups(1 pt)		16 oz	473 ml
3 cups		24 oz	710 ml
4 cups		32 oz	946 ml(1 L)

Weights

grams $\times$ 0.035 = ounces
ounces $\times$ 28.35 = grams

pounds	ounces	grams*
	$\frac{1}{4}$ oz	6 g
	$\frac{1}{2}$ oz	15 g
	1 oz	30 g
	1$\frac{3}{4}$ oz	50 g
	2 oz	60 g
	3 oz	90 g
$\frac{1}{4}$ lb	4 oz	120 g
	6 oz	170 g
$\frac{1}{2}$ lb	8 oz	230 g
$\frac{3}{4}$ lb	12 oz	340 g
1 lb	16 oz	450 g
1$\frac{1}{2}$ lbs	24 oz	685 g
2 lbs	32 oz	900 g

*equivalent

Linear Measures

inches $\times$ 2.54 = centimeters
centimeters $\times$ 0.39 = inches

inches	centimeters (millimeters)
$\frac{1}{4}$ "	5-6 mm
$\frac{3}{8}$ "	1 cm
$\frac{1}{2}$ "	1.5 cm
$\frac{3}{4}$ "	2 cm
1 "	2.5 cm
2 "	5 cm
4 "	10 cm
10 "	25 cm
12 "	30 cm
20 "	50 cm

Temperatures

$$\text{Fahrenheit} = \frac{\text{Celsius} \times 9}{5} + 32$$

$$\text{Celsius} = \frac{(\text{Fahrenheit} - 32) \times 5}{9}$$

DEEP-FRYING OIL TEMPERATURES
300°F-330°F(150°C-165°C) low
340°F-350°F(170°C-175°C) medium
350°F-360°F(175°C-180°C) high

Cup Conversions

1 cup whole basil leaves	1$\frac{3}{4}$ oz (50 g)
1 cup chopped basil	2 oz (60 g)
1 cup bean sprouts	3 oz (90 g)
1 cup cabbage, finely shredded	2$\frac{1}{2}$ oz (70 g)
1 cup all purpose flour	4 oz (120 g)
1 cup rice flour	6 oz (170 g)
1 cup long-grain rice (raw)	7 oz (200 g)
1 cup soybean paste	10 oz (285 g)

Abbreviations

Tbsp = tablespoon(s)   t = teaspoon(s)
oz = ounce(s)   g = grams   lb(s) = pound(s)
fl = fluid   ml = milliliter   L= liter
pt(s)=pint(s)   qt(s) = quart(s)
cm = centimeters   mm = millimeters

I N D E X

I N D E X